Tom Sheppard

Hull's Great Collector

by
Tim Schadla-Hall

Highgate Publications (Beverley) Ltd
1989

Acknowledgements

Gratitude is expressed for kind donations to assist the publication of *Tom Sheppard: Hull's Great Collector* from: C. W. and E. V. Wright, in memory of their friend and mentor, Tom Sheppard, and the Alec-Smith Charitable Trust Fund.

Illustrations

Gratitude is expressed to Hull Museums and Art Galleries for permission to reproduce all the photographs included in this publication.

Published by Highgate Publications (Beverley) Ltd.
24 Wylies Road, Beverley, HU17 7AP
Telephone (0482) 866826

Printed and Typeset in 10 on 11pt. Plantin by
B.A. press, 2-4 Newbegin, Lairgate, Beverley, HU17 8EG Telephone (0482) 882232

ISBN 0-948929-22-7

British Library Cataloguing in Publication Data
Schadla-Hall, R. T.
Tom Sheppard: Hull's great collector.
1. Humberside. Hull. Museums. Hull Museum. Sheppard, Thomas, 1876-1945
I. Title
069'.092'.4

ISBN 0-948929-22-7

Cover picture — Tom Sheppard
Cover picture — Hull Municipal Museum (Roy...

The Early Days

When Thomas Sheppard was appointed curator of Hull's Municipal Museum in 1901 he was 24 years old and had no previous experience of running or developing museums. In some ways he might not appear to have been an ideal candidate. Born at South Ferriby in North Lincolnshire on 2 October 1876 he had been educated in Hull through to elementary standard. He was the eldest of a family of 10 and left school as soon as possible, becoming a railway clerk in the manager's office at the Goods Station in Kingston Street, and later the Dock Offices (now the Town Docks Museum). A plaque has been placed on 5 Victoria Avenue, the home of the Sheppard family before their move to 432 Holderness Road. With his wife and son he later lived at 353 Anlaby Road, and, after the house was bombed in the war, moved to 46 Anlaby Park Road.

By the time he was appointed, however, he had already shown considerable ability as a field geologist; he had joined the Hull Geological Society in 1893, had been elected a Fellow of the Geological Society in 1900, and was secretary of the Hull Scientific and Field Naturalists' Club in 1898. His first published papers on geological subjects appeared in 1895, and his first book, *Geological Rambles in East Yorkshire,* was published in 1903. He was not only a good field geologist, but was obviously concerned with clear explanation and systematic presentation — both important to the good running of a museum.

Sheppard took over the old Hull Literary and Philosophical Museum in Albion Street, which had been acquired by the Corporation largely so that they could build an art gallery cheaply on top of the museum, and, as he later observed, this irreparably ruined the natural lighting in the existing museum. Originally the money for the art gallery was found from public subscription and there was little other income for the museum — indeed Sheppard was instructed on appointment 'that the museum was merely a means of obtaining an art gallery, that [he] could come at ten, smoke [his] cigar, leave when [he] liked, answer any enquiries that were necessary, look after the specimens, but on no account spend money, as it was required for the pictures'!

He later commented that 'in those days the salary did not encourage the cigar smoking habit' (in fact, his salary appears to have been £150 p.a., and the expenditure on all wages, rent, fittings, heating and lighting was approximately £100 p.a.). 'However, I managed to be about £250 in debt the first year, a habit which has been more or less chronic ever since, excepting on one memorable year, when, as very occasionally happens, the question of an increase in salary arose. I was told by my chairman, that if I had the money in hand at the year end, there would be no difficulty. By holding over rent accounts, and by other temporary measures, we actually had a balance in hand on the following year, but as I did not get my advance

Tom Sheppard, very much an extrovert, 'snapped' wearing tropical head-dress as he arrived at his office during a heat-wave in June, 1938.

Tom Sheppard on his appointment as Curator of Hull Municipal Museum.

Tom Sheppard on Hull Geological Society trip to Withernsea.

of salary and the balance in hand was lost to the committee and put in the general melting pot, I received a lesson which I have never forgotten.'

Sheppard had to take over a badly run-down museum. As a boy he had often visited the 'Lit and Phil' by paying one penny, and frequently found himself the only occupant. He was determined to change all this, and spent 18 months entirely redisplaying the collection, examining and cataloguing it. The museum was reopened on 2 June 1902, and the *Eastern Morning News* correspondent commented on the brightness of the new displays and also on the clarity of presentation. Better still, the museum, with free admission, was a great success — in the first week there were 1,700 visitors, in the second 1,900, and at the end of the year well over 2,000 per week. The city of Hull was very late, by comparison with other northern cities, in developing municipal museums, but it was certainly successful. By 1902 Sheppard had successfully persuaded the committee to open the museum two evenings a week from 7.30 p.m. to 9.30 p.m., from October to April, provided figures could be kept up, and, sure enough, they were, frequently numbering over 500 per evening. Later on, in 1908, the museums were opened on Sunday afternoons.

Views on Museums

Free, Informative, Relevant

Sheppard clearly stated what he expected his museum to do. He robustly criticised those museums which exhibited, or tried to exhibit 'objects of any and every description from all quarters of the globe', as he remarked: 'A Chinaman's hat, a lion's claw, a piece of Queen Elizabeth's walking stick, a double-headed pig, a stone from Jerusalem *etc. etc.* are all very well in their way, and may amuse a certain class of the community for the time being, but what good can a glance at scores and scores of such miscellaneous objects, crowded together in cases, do to those who have the fortune, or misfortune, to pass through the building?' He railed against those museums which contained 'collections of deformities, monstrosities and curios', admitting that, 'to some there is no doubt that an eight-legged lamb or a murderer's knife excites more interest than any other sort of exhibit.'

His firmly-held view was that most specimens in the museum should come from within the district. Although it becomes clear from later events that he found it hard to restrict himself to East Yorkshire and Hull, he stressed that no effort should be spared to make the collections 'more representative of the East Riding of Yorkshire than has been the case in the past', and he was always concerned to keep things locally. With the opening of his new museum he pointed out that 'there is now no good reason why valuable objects found in the neighbourhood should be sent to museums and collections elsewhere... within recent years many specimens of altogether exceptional interest have been forwarded to London and other places, some even out of the country altogether and irrevocably lost, so far as bringing them back to Hull is concerned.' He felt strongly that material from the area should be provided for local people to see, and he spent much time, without success, trying to regain material from the British Museum which he felt should be held locally.

Sheppard believed that musuems should primarily have an educational and improving role within the community — and gave hundreds of lectures to parties of schoolchildren which he advertised widely. He saw the role of the museum in providing people with a sense of place, and pride in their area, and the value of museums in attracting people to visit the city, frequently stressing in his annual reports the incidence of visitors from elsewhere in the country and abroad.

LECTURES
TO THE WORKING CLASSES

Hull Literary and Philosophical Society,

ROYAL INSTITUTION, ALBION-STREET.

THE

MUSEUM

IS OPEN TO THE PUBLIC

Every Saturday Afternoon

FROM ONE TO SIX O'CLOCK.

ADMISSION ONE PENNY.

SHORT LECTURE AT THREE O'CLOCK.

The attendance of Artisans, their Wives, and others is particularly desired.

A. K. ROLLIT, President.
T. M. EVANS, } Hon. Secs
B. CARLILL,

On SATURDAY, AUG. 3rd, 1878.

AT THREE O'CLOCK,

WM. STEPHENSON, ESQ., M.R.C.S.,

(OF BEVERLEY,)

WILL LECTURE ON

"The Yorkshire Wolds in Pre-Historic Times."

N.B.—A GEOLOGY SECTION is being formed; also a BOTANY CLASS (for Ladies), conducted by Mr. NIVEN, Curator of the Botanic Gardens; also a PUBLIC READING CLASS, under Mr. CHAS. JUDGE. Names may be given to the Curator.

Donations or Loans to the Museum of Articles of ingenuity or curiosity are solicited.

The MUSEUM will be OPEN to the Public on the Bank Holiday, MONDAY, August 5th. Admission One Penny.

Tom Sheppard was always keen to make museums more popular with the public.

Tom Sheppard — a typical pose, showing his knowledge and enthusiasm.

At a time of publicity about sightings of the Loch Ness monster, Tom Sheppard, a great man for publicity, created a local monster's footprint as a joke at Spurn Point.

8

The Collections

The key to his success, apart from his clear and forthright views, lay in his undoubted ability as a collector — modern museum ethics would have been anathema to Sheppard. He noted that, in his early memories of the 'Lit and Phil' museum, 'a fair proportion of the specimens [were] labelled as "lent by" Mr., Mrs. or Miss, Captain, Colonel, or Doctor so and so.' This problem was solved when the art gallery was being constructed on top of the Albion Street museum for, as he later explained, during construction the work was left incomplete and 'the "elements" played havoc with the specimens below. I suppose during that time the "lent by" labels were washed off; when I finally re-arranged the collection, there was not one left, and I will say that it is to the credit of the people of Hull to report that, with one exception, there has never been an application for any object said to have been on loan.' One cannot help feeling that the most important of the 'elements' which Sheppard mentions was himself. He cheerfully admitted that before 1913 he had been approached by a 'well-known professor of the Leeds University' who greeted him with the remark, 'Well, Sheppard, and how's thieving?'

He became an accomplished collector, and in 1923 an after-dinner speech at a function at which Sheppard was present included the comment: 'it was conveyed to us that the Hull Curator had filled his museums and store rooms by the laudable exercise of [the] same traits [as Viking raiders], having, like William the Conqueror, an ingrained habit of annexing objects first and asking, or not asking, permission as seemed expedient afterwards … a habit which is believed to have reduced to despair the authorities of other musuems within Mr Sheppard's sphere of influence, who, with a due respect for red tape and the conventions, found themselves handicapped in the race for the acquisition of rare finds and valuable ethnological specimens.'

Sheppard was loved and feared by his fellow workers, and at the time of his retirement received a wonderful tribute from T. D. Kendrick, Keeper of Prehistoric and Medieval Antiquities at the British Museum: 'I can at least say that the mere record of your achievements, as known to all of us, is in itself a fine and stimulating example to your brother-curators, and I feel it would not be over-pretentious to claim that, as a result of your long and energetic labours, you have conspicuously contributed to the general enrichment of the English heritage.' But he then went on: 'I cannot personally pay you a higher compliment than to say that I have always been very thankful that you and I never desperately wanted the same object!' Finally he made a generous offer: 'It is impossible to think of your collecting activities ceasing entirely, and I needn't say that you will always find us, wherever you are, very ready to help you in any matters concerning British antiquities; always providing, of course, that you are not actually engaged

Tom Sheppard casts a professional eye over the collection.

in snatching them away from under my nose!' Sheppard, by then, was retired, and not finding life exactly congenial, but, in his reply to Kendrick, he had time to refer to his successor whom he clearly felt fell far short of his own standards: 'He has promised not to purchase anything nor incur any expenses in the way of printing *etc.* (for the duration of the war) — it will suit the Committee! He has even refused gifts which I should have jumped at!'

Sheppard also purchased material for the museum, but his correspondence with the British Museum, where he frequently sought advice, clearly indicates a marked reluctance to spend more than he needed to, and he always hoped for gifts rather than purchases. Apart from frequenting salerooms, he also developed a series of contacts throughout Yorkshire and Lincolnshire, and 'combed the local newspapers every morning for references to archaeological or other discoveries; if a flint axe was reported as found in North Yorkshire a telegraphed offer of a fiver from Sheppard would often secure it for Hull before the local museum had woken up to the discovery.' On another occasion 'a Bronze Age beaker was found in fragments at Elloughton in the garden of Mr. Alfred McIlwaine.

Sheppard was asked to identify it and duly reconstructed it — but he also prepared a copy and offered a choice to McIlwaine, who claimed to have chosen the original'.

Above all, Sheppard collected for Hull and its area, often stressing the point that the specimens were 'in the possession of the public' and that, because 'the collections were in the custody of the Corporation, the permanent safety of the contents was assured'. He also passionately defended the need for *free* access to museums, and attacked the art gallery for initially charging — stressing that culture and heritage should be available to all parts of the community. The only group which was excluded from Albion Street in its early days were small boys with dirty shoes or an untidy appearance, who were firmly banned by Sheppard's faithful ally, Edmund Raper, the first museum attendant.

It is impossible to list all of Sheppard's acquisitions. He successfully begged most of the material which makes up the whaling and fishing displays; he cajoled local builders and developers to part with fragments and often whole sections of buildings; he persuaded the local societies, particularly the Hull Geological Society and the East Riding Antiquarian Society, to gift their collections to his museum (in these cases he was closely associated with both organizations); and he often befriended individuals, who later showed their great generosity.

The Mortimer Collection

In some cases Sheppard wished to acquire collections which he could not afford. Even before he had been appointed Curator he had written of the need to safeguard the Mortimer Collection at Driffield, and he campaigned intermittently for 13 years to get it into the City's museums. The Mortimer Collection was housed in a purpose-built museum in Driffield, and represented the life's work of J. R. and Robert Mortimer, corn merchants in Driffield, and, more importantly, originators of a vast local archaeological and geological collection. The collections comprised at least 66,000 specimens, of which 60,000 were archaeological and 6,000 geological. The bulk of the archaeological material had been excavated and collected by the Mortimer brothers from mainly Bronze Age burial mounds and other archaeological sites in the East Riding of Yorkshire, and represented by 1900, as J. R. Mortimer pointed out, one of only three out of 18 local archaeological collections which had not left the area. In 1900 J. R. Mortimer was already worrying about the future. 'Surely,' he wrote, 'the East Riding possesses some governing body which, before it is too late, will see the wisdom of permanently possessing [the collections], and handing

Opening of the Mortimer Collection.

them down to future governing bodies as a source of education and a treasure of permanent value to the district.'

Sheppard had already met and talked to Mortimer (as he had to the other great local antiquary, Canon Greenwell) well before Mortimer wrote of his concern. Indeed, Sheppard had spent a great deal of time with him and even published part of the collection for 1900. Sheppard became a close friend of Mortimer and was instrumental in producing *Forty Years Researches in the British and Saxon Burial Mounds of East Yorkshire*, the great volume on the Mortimers' collection. It is clear that he was involved with the production of the volume and effectively edited it, as well as seeing it through the presses to its final publication in 1905. Sheppard probably knew the collections better than anyone else.

On J. R. Mortimer's death in 1911 the Trustees of the museum at Driffield were instructed by the terms of Mortimer's will to try and keep the collection in Driffield. If they failed, 'Hull had a year's opportunity of purchasing the collection from the Trustees. Driffield having failed to

12

conform to the conditions, Hull had an opportunity' to acquire the material. Sheppard failed to negotiate what he considered to be a reasonable price with the Trustees, who had originally sought £3,000. There was a great deal of negotiation and, even though Sheppard's first committee chairman and supporter, Alderman John Brown, wielded considerable power, and was mayor in 1913, it seemed the city would not pay for the collection. Sheppard attacked the City Council for its parsimony in the newspapers (no local government officer would risk that today!), but still with no result. It appears that Sheppard managed to gain agreement to a new price of £1,000, provided the collections were exhibited in a building intact, not mixed up with general collections, and called 'The Mortimer Collection'. It was at this point that Colonel G. H. Clarke, a close ally of Sheppard, 'handsomely came forward and provided the necessary money', and the collection finally passed to the Corporation.

The First World War followed hard on the heels of the purchase, and there was a shortage of money and a lack of transport, which held up the movement of the collections from Driffield to Hull. Sheppard had considerable difficulty in moving the collection at all, but in the end he managed in 1916 to convince the Corporation that the collections would be safer removed from Driffield, where American troops might want the museum building at 12 hours notice. He still had problems with transport, but the City Engineer made available a steam lorry and trailer and the whole task was completed over several weeks in something like 20 loads. Packing cases were also hard to find, but, as Sheppard tells it: 'Luckily I had a friend at a local brewery and, after frequent and pleasant visits thereto, I managed to borrow about two hundred boxes, each of which held a dozen of whisky once.'

The process of cataloguing was a lengthy one which was to take several years, and the problem of finding a home to conform with the agreement reached with the Trustees was considerable. The generosity of T. R. Ferens in providing the present Ferens Art Gallery for the city meant, however, that the old Art Gallery at the rear of the City Hall was vacant, and on 1 October 1929 Sir Frederic G. Kenyon, KCB, LLD, D.Litt., Director of the British Museum, opened the new displays; Colonel Clarke gave the civic party luncheon in the City Hall. It had taken 16 years to get the collections on display in Hull from the time that Sheppard first suggested it — another example of his great tenacity.

It seems worth mentioning that, although the official announcement of the purchase of the collections was made in July 1913, Sheppard had already written to Reginald Smith at the British Museum on 12 May 1913 as follows: 'Did I tell you we had the Driffield Collection offered for a thousand pounds and a Hull gentleman has found the money?' This can only indicate the amount of manipulation in which Sheppard was involved in obtaining the collection and keeping other potential purchasers well away.

The Anglo-Japanese Exhibition of 1910

It would take many volumes to document all Sheppard's collecting coups, for he never missed a chance. One excellent example of his *modus operandi* is provided by his acquisition of a large number of exhibits from the Anglo-Japanese exhibition in London. In September 1910 he 'received a letter from N. Kasuga Esq., member of the Imperial Bureau of Fisheries, Tokio, Japan, and the representative of the Fisheries Section of the Anglo-Japanese exhibition, London, offering a model of the Japanese fisheries exhibited at the exhibition.'

Sheppard went to London and, having discovered from one of the Commissioner's assistants that the Commissioner was 'inundated with letters' from other museums 'asking the Commissioner to describe the proffered models. What size were they? Were they on stands or in cases? Could he arrange to have them packed? What would the cost be, the carriage, insurance *etc. etc.*?', he obtained an audience with the Commissioner, compiled a catalogue of *all* the exhibits not apportioned, and offered to save the Commissioner 'from any more trouble or anxiety by bringing men to pack and remove the specimens at once.' Sheppard tells the story perfectly; 'After some hesitation the Commissioner kindly presented all the collection, not apportioned, to Hull Corporation, on behalf of the Japanese government, and even went to the extent of allowing me to bring one or two further interesting exhibits away "by mistake".' Once again Thomas Sheppard received a major collection at virtually no cost to the Corporation.

The Brigg Boat

Sheppard had always operated at great speed. In April 1909 he wrote to the owner of the Brigg boat, Mr. V. Cary-Elwes, suggesting that this important Lincolnshire find, the largest log boat ever found in Europe, should be moved from Brigg, where Mr. Cary-Elwes had placed it in a building specifically constructed for its exhibition and be taken to Hull Museum. Sheppard had previously asked and been told 'no', but, on the second occasion, the owner agreed. 'Mr. Sheppard immediately got the services of a "break-down gang" from the City Engineer, and without delay the boat was put on a keel bound for Hull. The next day the owner, having reconsidered the matter, wired, "Do not move boat" ', but Mr. Sheppard was able to wire back, almost truthfully: 'Boat already in Hull', and it remained there until it was destroyed in 1943.

The Museum in Albion Street was used by Thornton-Varley Ltd. after their premises had been bombed.

The Brigg boat in Hull Municipal Museum, Albion Street.

Collecting Museums

When Thomas Sheppard was appointed Curator of the Albion Street Museum, or Hull's Municipal Museum as it was known officially, no one seems to have thought it likely that by 1941, on his retirement, the City would boast effectively nine museums. The creation of an additional eight museums over a period of 40 years was his greatest achievement.

During the period of his employment by the City the following museums were opened:

The Municipal Museum in Albion Street, opened to the public on 2 June 1902.

Wilberforce House, High Street, opened to the public as Hull's historical museum, on 24 August 1906.

The opening of Wilberforce House and its subsequent development was in many ways Sheppard's greatest achievement. Alderman Brown, Sheppard's first committee chairman, had already acquired part of the building from the Corporation before 1901, and was able, with support

Hull Municipal Museum, Albion Street, Antiquities Gallery.

The Georgian Room, Wilberforce House, as it was in Tom Sheppard's time.

The Georgian Room, Wilberforce House, today.

from Sheppard, to persuade the Corporation to purchase the whole of the building shortly after his appointment. Sheppard spent a great deal of time acquiring an unrivalled collection of material connected with William Wilberforce and the abolition of slavery, and he later developed a series of period rooms with the help of many generous local benefactors.

Natural History Museum (in the old Art Gallery), Albion Street, opened to the public on 12 November 1910.

In one sense this was hardly the opening of a new museum. All it meant was 'moving upstairs' at Albion Street, for, as a result of the generosity of T. R. Ferens MP, it proved possible to build a new art gallery at the rear of the City Hall, thus vacating the premises above the Albion Street museum, which Sheppard had previously complained had ruined the lighting of the original museum. By 1910 there were ample collections available to fill the now empty galleries.

The Museum of Fisheries and Shipping, Pickering Park, opened to the public on 30 March 1912.

Sheppard had inherited a number of important exhibits from the original 'Lit and Phil' museum, and engaged himself from the time of his appointment in amassing as much material as possible on fisheries and whaling, mainly by the process of begging both locally and nationally. The collections by 1910 had reached almost unmanageable proportions, but Christopher Pickering, a local trawler owner and philanthropist, eventually provided a purpose-built museum building which was to be the most popular of Hull's museums for many years.

The Museum of Commerce and Transport, High Street, opened on 1 May 1925.

This museum was one of Sheppard's most original ideas and certainly caught the public's imagination. It was sited in the old Corn Exchange (now the Archaeology and Transport Museum) in High Street. Sheppard envisaged opening 'the first permanent commercial museum in the country', and persuaded a large number of local firms to exhibit a selection of their products and explain their industrial processes. The local companies not only paid for their exhibits but also for the cases in which they were placed. The building contained a number of models, including one of the dock frontage of the city, and also a number of items which Sheppard had already collected relating to transport in Hull and its surroundings. He also acquired, from the Wembley Exhibition of 1924, a number of other exhibits relating to transport, and was able to acquire an important group of early motorcars from the first motor museum in London via the Science Museum. To this was added a number of horse-drawn vehicles which were begged from all over the country. For the rest of his career, he continued to add to this museum, which eventually boasted a sea plane which hung from the ceiling.

Museum of Fisheries and Shipping.

The Museum in Albion Street.

Museum of Fisheries and Shipping.

21

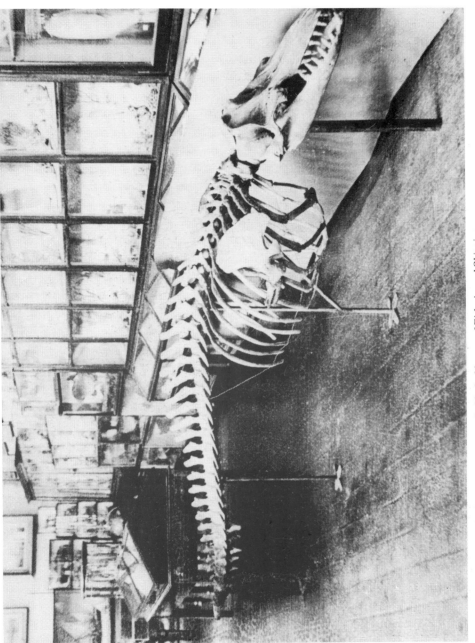

Inside the Museum of Fisheries and Shipping.

Tom Sheppard sharing his knowledge with interested onlookers.

As usual Tom Sheppard quickly at the scene of a recently discovered well.

The Tithe Barn Museum, Easington, opened to the public on 4 October 1928.

Sheppard had long been concerned with the fate of what he called 'bygones' and what we today would probably call Social History material. He bemoaned the loss of the old buildings from the old town of Hull as well as the disappearance of rural crafts and rural buildings, and as early as 1913 had pleaded for a folk-lore museum in an East Hull park. Certainly by 1923 he was advocating that 'a collection of old buildings worthy of preservation' should be 'gathered together ... in one of the parks', and mentioned that 'we have an old tithe barn in this district which I am hoping may shortly be preserved'. This building was, of course, the tithe barn at Easington, which, strictly speaking, never became part of the Corporation's full responsibility. It was run by the East Riding Antiquarian Society and filled with Hull Corporation's collections, which were provided by Sheppard. The displays were developed under Sheppard's guidance, but the museum did not survive his retirement. This seems to be the only museum which he failed to 'pull off'.

The Mortimer Collection of Prehistoric Antiquities, purchased for the Corporation by Colonel G. H. Clarke in 1913 and opened to the public on 1 October 1929.

This was the second old art gallery which Sheppard was able to take over from the museums as a result of the generosity of T. R. Ferens. Ferens had provided the money for the present art gallery, and the space vacated at the rear of the City Hall was ideal not only for the display of the Mortimer Collection, but also provided a series of temporary exhibition galleries where Sheppard was able to encourage local societies and other organisations to put on exhibitions at the rate of about six a year.

The Railway Museum, Paragon Station, opened on 24 February 1933.

Thomas Sheppard started work with North Eastern Railway and had always been an avid collector of material relating to railway history. The increasingly crowded Commerce and Transport Museum had little space for the range of exhibits and models which he had accumulated, and in 1933 the North Eastern Railway provided and decorated a room over the left luggage office at Paragon Station which Sheppard duly filled with his exhibits. It is said that, shortly after the opening of the musuem, the 'Railway Museum' was added to the letter head of Sheppard's notepaper, and one of the first things he did was write to the North Eastern Railway suggesting he was given a free rail pass as he was now involved in the collection of railway memorabilia!

Hull's 'Old Time' street museum, never officially opened to the public.

By 1901 Thomas Sheppard had begun to collect parts of buildings from the old town of the city and had written widely bemoaning the loss of the historic core of the old town. As early as 1935 he wrote of his intention to

Corn Exchange, High Street, which later became the Museum of Commerce and Transport.

The scene at the banquet held at the opening of the Corn Exchange, High Street, later the Museum of Commerce and Transport. (from the Illustrated London News).

Museum of Commerce and Transport.

Museum of Commerce and Transport: acquiring a seaplane.

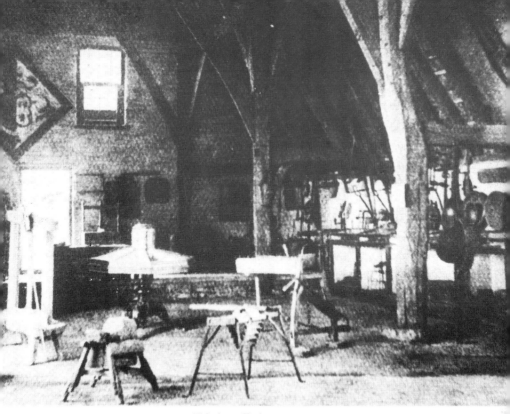

Tithe barn, Easington.

Tom Sheppard's old street, destroyed in the blitz.

Old Time Street: King's Head.

rebuild a number of shop and building fronts in a large warehouse at the rear of Wilberforce House, and, by working steadily with his loyal band of assistants, he was able to show the part-finished museum to selected parties. A number of old buildings, including the King's Head public house, a chemist's shop, a tobacconist's, a wood turner's and a blacksmith's shop, as well as the White Lion hotel, were all painstakingly re-erected, and material was acquired from further afield, such as the fine shop front from Lewes in Sussex. He was engaged in creating a cobbled street, and already had vehicles placed upon it as well as quantities of street furniture. Sheppard always claimed that this remarkable museum was his own idea, and its subsequent destruction in half-finished state was a sad loss to the City for, had it remained, today it would in many ways have been a more authentic local street than the famous street at the York Castle Museum.

Running the Museums

Sheppard never had a large staff to run and ward his museums. Indeed he apparently saw no need for one. In 1923 he said that 'he did not think the question of extra costs of administration affected [the Corporation; in spite of all the museums] he would see to it that they did not appoint curators to each museum', and he pointed out that at 'Wilberforce House Museum, where there were 15 rooms and only one attendant, as far as he knew, nothing more than a thermometer had disappeared during 14 years'. Times have changed.

In 1906 he listed his total staff as T. Stainforth, assistant (Albion Street), E. J. Raper, attendant (Albion Street), F. J. Lockyear, clerk (Wilberforce House) and W. Bartley, attendant (Wilberforce House). As late as 1938 the professional staff of the museum comprised the late J. B. Fay, Assistant Director, J. B. Thirsk, who was a clerk and recorder for much of Sheppard's career, the late W. H. Southern, and A. K. Wallis. This small and loyal band sustained the museums right up to the outbreak of the Second World War.

Not only was the staff small, but the total budget for the enterprises which Sheppard embarked upon was also extremely limited, and it appears that he was always short of funds. In 1913, at the Museums Association Conference held in Hull, he mentioned the shortage of finance over the early period of the museums' development: 'There is little wonder that at the end of the first year [1901] the expenditure exceeded income. This has been a chronic complaint with us ever since, though just now the chairman is probably effectively putting the screw on by threatening to knock it off', and he then added, 'This year we shall probably be better off as I am not having any expenses for attending a museums conference.' All this was presumably said in front of his chairman, and then subsequently printed for all to read!

He seems to have been involved in a constant battle to extract limited sums from the Corporation. For example, in 1928 he wrote to Reginald Smith at the British Museum to ask if it was possible to purchase a separate copy of Smith's paper on Bronze Age Hammers which had appeared in a recent volume of *Archaeologia;* 'I have been trying to purchase the volume but understand that it will cost £5-5s.-0 and my committee will not go to that expense.'

Retirement

Thomas Sheppard retired reluctantly on 30 September 1941, 'having reached the age of 65 when retirement on a pension was compulsory'. For a brief period there was some uncertainty as to whether he would not be re-engaged as Director of Museums for the duration of the war, but this was not to be. His health broke down shortly after his retirement, and he died on 20 February 1945. His last years cannot have been happy ones: with his

Tom Sheppard and his staff.
Tom Sheppard expounding on the museum collection.

retirement Hull Corporation's interest in his beloved Tithe Barn museum ceased; his 'Old Time' Street museum was destroyed by the 1941 air raids, incomplete and never officially opened to the public; the Mortimer Collections were removed from display as a result of the same period of air raids; and in June 1943 the Albion Street museum was gutted by incendiaries with the subsequent loss of virtually all that was in the building. Much of his life's work was lost and yet much still survives in the present work of the museums where the rest of his collections are still the backbone of what is displayed.

He was a remarkable man, outspoken and honest in public. He seems to have enjoyed reminiscing about his career; for example, in 1913 he retold the story of his appointmernt in 1901: 'After what seemed to be a very long delay, applications were invited for the post of curator, and one of our experts and myself were selected as candidates. Possibly because I knew least about museums, I was appointed.' He could well afford to joke about his position in public, for by then he had opened three museums and the Mortimer Collection was almost his. His sense of humour was matched by his readiness to help anyone with an interest. E. V. Wright recently described how he and his elder brother, C. W. Wright, joined Sheppard 'in expeditions to sites of interest which we should have not otherwise have found or known about', and he described how on one trip Sheppard took them to Barton and onto the old railway track where he 'showed them how, as a boy, he and his friends and brothers used to move at a good pace balanced on the rails.' He was a regular and entertaining speaker, providing a fund of lectures to schoolchildren and adults alike on a vast range of subjects, and gave 'unstintingly of his time to encourage people in pursuit of studies in the many fields spanned by his well-filled mind.' He had made friends and supporters and he was a personal friend of Colette O'Neill, the actress, and Marie Stopes, the campaigner for birth control. Indeed his range of friends seems to have been as great as his range of knowledge.

Sheppard the Author and Editor

He was a prodigious correspondent, although sadly the destruction of the Albion Street museum resulted in the apparent destruction of most of his correspondence. It seems, as an example, that he wrote on average 50 letters a year to the British Museum and this was no doubt matched with his correspondence to other institutions. His constant thirst for knowledge and his desire to produce a wide range of papers on a variety of subjects made him well-known nationally and internationally.

His output of published papers was quite outstanding and his products turned up not only in learned academic journals but also in dental

Tom Sheppard in Copenhagen.
Tom Sheppard at his desk.

magazines. In the period 1901-41, 213 museum publications appeared, all edited by him, and, in the majority of cases, also written by him. These publications not only documented the collections but also described the museums which he developed and were as low priced as possible to make them available to the public. As well as writing on a wide variety of subjects and expanding the history of Hull, he also edited *The Naturalist* for 30 years and the *Transactions of the East Riding Antiquarian Society* for a similar period. He was also editor of the *Transactions of the Hull Geological Society* and the *Transactions of the Hull Scientific and Field Naturalists Club.* He wrote a large number of books, and many of his papers were republished as independent volumes later. His better-known books include *Geological Rambles in East Yorkshire, The Evolution of Kingston upon Hull, The Lost Towns of the Yorkshire Coast, The Bibliography of Yorkshire Geology, Yorkshire Past and Present, Yorkshire's Contribution to Science* and *The Correct Arms of Hull.* There is little doubt that, in addition to his own writing and editing of journals, he was also largely responsible for ensuring the publication and the presentation of J. R. Mortimer's great book, *Forty Years Researches in the British and Saxon Burial Mounds of East Yorkshire.*

In academic terms Sheppard probably saw himself primarily as a geologist, (although this should not detract from his work in other fields) and it was for his work in the field of geology that he received his honorary M.Sc. from the University of Leeds. Nonetheless, it is difficult not to think of him as the complete polymath. Apart from being president of the Yorkshire Geological Society, and the Yorkshire Naturalists Union, the Museums Association, the Hull Geological Society, and the Yorkshire Numismatic Society, he was also vice-president of the Hull Shakespeare Society, president of the Hull Playgoers Society and chairman of the Hull Repertory Theatre Ltd.

'A persuasive geniality was his outstanding characteristic. He converted many hard headed vendors into generous donors and made the giver of a single coin or fossil feel that he was making a real contribution to science.' It is difficult to summarise a man who achieved so much, who started life with an elementary education yet gained an M.Sc., who was quite remarkable as an individual, as an academic and as a museum curator. His lasting monument is still represented by Hull museums and his robust championship of the cause of those museums, based on his belief in free public access to the benefit of all, remains a great example.

'In Hull we take second place to none for the opinion we hold of the value of the work our museums are doing; and we consider this is amply borne out by the magnificent way in which our efforts are supported by the public, and especially by the many friends who have in such a practical manner shown that they appreciate what is being done.'

Thomas Sheppard, July 1913.

36

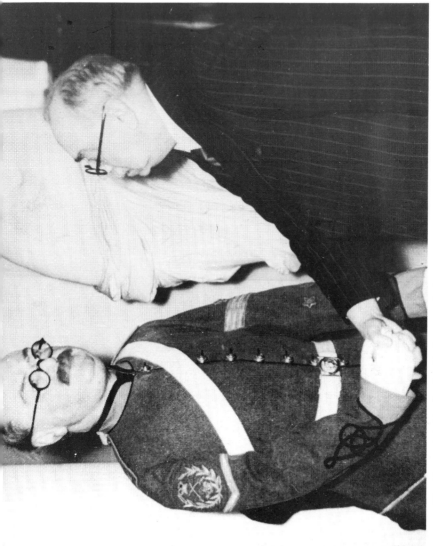

Tom Sheppard shaking hands with the waxwork model of himself which he aquired from Madame Tussaud's so that it could watch over his museum after his retirement.

37

Tom Sheppard: a caricature.